George to Town

Carolyn Sloan
Illustrated by David Sheldon

Rigby
A Harcourt Achieve Imprint

www.Rigby.com
1-800-531-5015

The day of the big move had arrived—
George Fry and his mom were leaving their
little house in the country for good. Their
moods couldn't have been more different.

"We're off to live in the city," said Mom,
with happiness.

"But Mom, we're leaving here," said
George, miserably.

He said his goodbyes to Mr. and Mrs. Benet who lived next door, and to their cat, Cashew, and their dog, Humbug. George couldn't imagine what life would be like without these friends.

In the backyard, George looked longingly at the summer rosebush he and Mom had planted and at the green tomatoes he had grown from seeds.

"I want to take my tomatoes with us," George declared.

"But, George, I told you, we won't have a garden," said Mom gently. "We're going to live in a high-rise apartment building with no backyard or garden, but it'll be like living up in the sky."

George wasn't sure how much fun he could have without a garden, without Cashew and Humbug, and without Mr. and Mrs. Benet next door.

"But I'll be the boy who lives in the sky, and that could be fun," he thought.

George and Mom drove behind the moving truck. George felt better once they had left the country and he couldn't see the things he had left behind. He made up a little song about himself—"I'm George Fry, and I live in the sky!"

When they finally arrived in the city, George explored the new apartment, still singing, "I'm George Fry who lives in the sky." Mom was pleased to see George had cheered up.

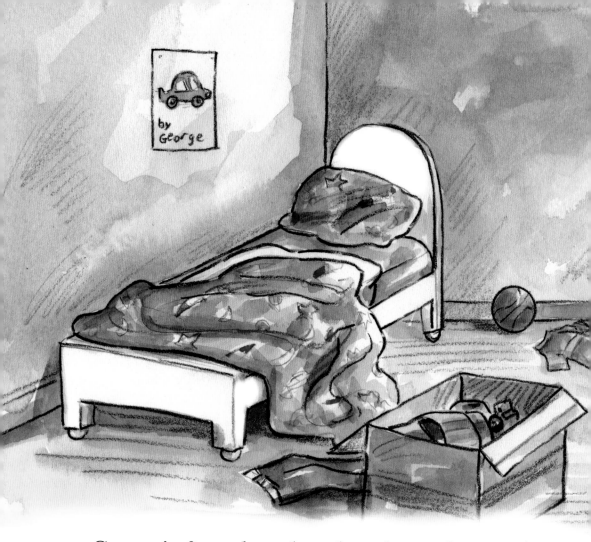

George's first thought when he woke up the next morning was that he'd go and play with Cashew and Humbug next door.

And then he remembered—there was no Cashew or Humbug next door. There was no Mr. or Mrs. Benet either.

George climbed out of his bed and peered
out the window. He could only see sky and
clouds and sometimes a bird or an airplane.
He had to climb on top of a box to see down
into the city far, far away.

Cars and trucks passed in the busy streets. George knew they made roaring noises and knew they smelled of gas and smoke, but up in his sky home, George could neither hear them nor smell them.

The people in the street looked like tiny little toy people.

"We're the 'up' people," said George to himself, "and they're the 'down' ones. Hey, 'down' people, look up and see me! I'm George Fry, and I live in the sky."

"When can we go out and meet people here?" George asked his mother later.

"Another day, George," said Mom, climbing up a ladder. There was so much painting to do and so many curtains to hang. "Don't worry, you'll soon make friends when you go to your new school next week."

George wandered around looking for
something to do. He'd already unpacked
his toys and arranged his car collection
on a shelf.

He wanted something—anything—to happen.
He was rarely bored in the country and
thought for sure he'd never be bored in the
busy city. "I'm George Fry, and I live in the
sky," he muttered, "and not a lot goes on
up here."

Then suddenly he knew what would help
him feel at home.

"Mom, can we get a dog?"

"I'm afraid not, George, because we're not allowed to keep pets here."

"A cat then . . . or a rat . . . or a camel . . . or . . ."

"Oh, George, don't be silly! No pets means no animals at all, OK? Now please hand me that blue paintbrush."

George gave his mom the paintbrush and let out a sigh as big as the wind at the start of a storm. He wanted to help his mom, but his mom said he was too small to hang curtains and not careful enough to help with painting.

"Why don't you paint a picture instead?" she suggested.

So George got out his paints, and he painted Cashew and Humbug. Then he made up a story about them:

Cashew and Humbug flew past my window in a big, bright balloon. When they saw me—George Fry who lives in the sky—they waved until the balloon basket rocked and rolled. I invited them in to a party I was having, and then . . .

George stopped and said to himself, "Yes, and then what?"

Then Cashew and Humbug flew off because there wasn't any party, and they couldn't get in anyway.

George sniffed unhappily.

"Are you OK, George?" asked Mom, who had heard the sniff.

"Yes," said George unconvincingly. He tried some more stories—one about a frog who went to a football game and another about a whale called Walter who got seasick.

A frog went to a football game.

There once was a whale.

Then he started a third one about a big, friendly giant called Maggie who had pink hair and colorful clothes and turned-up toes.

She had a smiley face and long, huggy arms, and George just loved Maggie. He liked her SO MUCH that he didn't want her to stay in his story.

"Come out of that story!" he whispered to the picture. "Come and stay with me and be my friend!"

And Maggie did just that because she was kind, and she wanted to be George's friend.

Maggie was a great friend because she brought George warm milk at bedtime, found missing pieces for his puzzles, and stayed with him when he was scared of the dark.

Day after day, George told his mom how much fun he and Maggie had together, so Mom didn't mind her staying.

"So Maggie can sleep in my room?"

"Yes, OK, George."

"And eat at the table with us?"

"If she wants to," said Mom as she
sat down.

"Not there, Mom," shouted George, "or
you'll squash Maggie!"

"Whoops, sorry," said Mom, "I didn't
see her!"

"How could you not see her when she's so
big?" George laughed.

"Er . . . yes, so she is," said Mom
wonderingly.

George was delighted when, at last, Mom said, "We're going out to the park today, just as soon as we finish shopping."

"Can Maggie come, too?" asked George.

"Of course she can!" said Mom, smiling at the sofa where she thought Maggie might be.

"You and I," George sang happily to Maggie, "live high in the sky!"

But when they went out, Maggie couldn't fit into the elevator–no matter how she squeezed and squashed.

"She'll have to go down all those stairs," sighed George.

So Mom and George took the elevator, and they waited at the bottom for Maggie to come. They waited and waited.

"Here she comes at last," said George, "but she looks worn out! We'll have to go very slowly for her, Mom."

Out and about, Maggie was a bit troublesome, getting stuck between carts at the supermarket and getting lost in the fiction section of the library, and then she was scared to go on an escalator.

"That Maggie really holds us up," Mom thought, "and she isn't even *there*!"

George and Maggie met some other children in the park. They played a game of freeze tag, and Maggie pushed them all on the swings.

However, George was very quiet when it was time to go home.

"Ready?" asked Mom.

"Yes," said George, staring at the ground.

"And is Maggie ready, too?"

"She's not coming," George muttered. "Can't you see?"

"See what, George?" Mom asked worriedly.

"She made some new friends. She decided to stay and play with them today."

"Oh, George, I'm so sorry."

"It's OK," said George, "because she was a bit big, and anyway, you didn't really see her, did you?"

Mom took George's hand and said gently, "Maybe I didn't see her like you did, but I knew she was there."

George made up more stories, hoping to find another friend. There was an ant in striped pants, a beetle that lived in a bottle, and a bear in the broom closet, but none of them were extra special like Maggie.

"School starts tomorrow," said Mom one day. George was excited because finally he could tell everyone at school how he was George Fry who lived in the sky, even if the sky was a bit of a lonely place where you couldn't keep pets.

George made lots of friends at school.

One day when Mom picked him up, she said, "Guess what I found out! It's only dogs and cats that we can't keep in the high-rise. So, surprise, surprise, what do you think I bought today?"

"An ant in striped pants," guessed George, "or a beetle in a bottle?"

"A bird," said Mom excitedly, "with red and yellow and blue feathers and a long tail!"

George thought, "This is almost as good as one of my stories!"

"And he's called Jester and he can *talk*!" Mom went on.

Now George *knew* she had made Jester up. When he got home, he would pretend he could see him, too.

But he didn't have to pretend! Jester was real, and he said, "Hello, sweetie-pie!" in a funny, croaky bird voice.

George took good care of Jester, played games with him, and taught him new words.

"Birds should live in the sky," he thought happily. He taught Jester his song and Jester sang it over and over—and out of tune—every day:

"George Fry and I live in the sky,
Live in the sky,
Live in the sky!"